Please Read

(if at all possible)

+ Thanks.

This Camera is obviously late.
I'm sorry.
I'm not sure what the arrival
policy is, but I hope it's not
Strict to the point of not
accepting my day-late mail-in.
But see, I don't even know
if it's a day late or many
days late, because I don't know
if it's the postmark that counts
or the day it arrives. I hope
it's the former... but even then

Jan. 31st was a Sunday, and mail is nonexistent on Sundays.

I'm sorry if I'm making very little sense. Basically, I found myself having a hard time picking things to take pictures of. I procrastinated and didn't even end up using the whole roll of film.

But... well... sorry. This project was important to me... I hope you can forgive, or make an exception.

Thank you for taking the time to read this.

— Jordan

In 2007 Kate Engelbrecht began sending cameras and questionnaires to teenage girls across the country. She asked them to use the camera to communicate their view of themselves and the world around them. The questionnaires were based on the famous Proust Questionnaire, aimed at revealing a person's true personality. Eventually, nearly 5,000 girls between the ages of 13 and 18 took part in the project. Girls from all parts of the country, of different backgrounds, faiths, and races, participated in what became known as The Girl Project. It is an account of teenage girlhood, experienced and communicated as only teenage girls know and understand.

Please Read (if at all possible)

The Girl Project
by Kate Engelbrecht

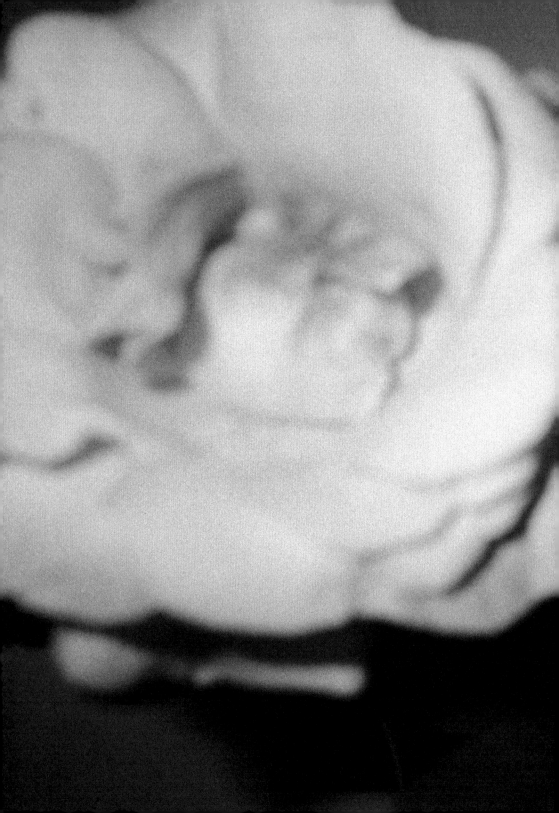

Answering the following questions is not required to participate in The Girl
Project, though I would really appreciate your comments. Be as specific as you
like. Send in with your camera and release form. Your name is not on this piece of
paper and will not be used in conjunction with your identity.

1.) What adjectives best describe you?

Artistic, fashionable, fun

2.) What is the hardest part about being a teenager?

The hardest part is learning how to grow up, and learning things/skills
you aren't taught in school, such as how to use a checkbook.

3.) What is the best part about being a teenager?

The best part is that you get to be young and have fun with hardly
any obligations or strings attached.

4.) What are your favorite qualities in a person?

My favorite qualities are honesty, the ability to have fun, respect
and love

5.) What is your idea of happiness?

My idea of happiness is the ability to appreciate what you already have,
to love and be loved by others, and most importantly, a meaning or goal in my life.

6.) What is your ideal profession?

My ideal profession is some career in the art field, a fashion designer maybe?

7.) Tell me one thing about you that nobody else seems to get?

Sometimes I feel like no one understands
my opinions or beliefs, or agrees with me fully.

8.) What is your favorite color? Purple

9.) If you could live anywhere in the world, where would you live?

I would live in Japan because I love their unique culture.

10.) What do you think about the way(s) that teenage girls are portrayed in our culture? In our culture, teenage girls are given the image of tall, perfect, skinny models who wear ridiculous amounts of make up. The truth is, hardly any girls look like the fake icons of our society. You see them as famous singers, or actresses, but never as just people.

11.) What are you afraid of? being unloved, being betrayed,
I'm afraid of being rejected, being unloved, being betrayed, or losing loved ones. I am afraid of being alone.

12.) What are you most proud of?
I am most proud of my artistic talents and grades in school.

13.) In as many or few words necessary, tell me about being you.

Being me is about living life. It's about making every moment of my precious life the best. It's about expressing myself through my art, and giving kindness to those around me. It's also about working towards goals, getting through the tough times, and making the world a better place. Being me is fun.

Dear Girl

Three years ago I became fascinated by popular depictions of you. I didn't recognize you. Bratty. Slutty. Spoiled. Vapid. Mean—even vicious. Absent of heart or soul. I didn't see myself in you or relate to you. After all, I didn't know any teenage girls anymore, and like so many adults, I understood you only through the media. I couldn't imagine how or why teenage girlhood had changed so much since my own adolescence.

I started The Girl Project as a way to explore my questions and confusion. And as the first cameras and questionnaires came in, it became clear, through your poignant photos and words, that you are not as you are so commonly portrayed.

This project has become less about my curiosity of you and more to do with making sure your lives get shared. Your lives are, in fact, deeply meaningful. I especially wish to share your lives with you—back to you—and with every other girl that turns these pages. Who you are, individually and collectively, is so much bigger than I or any other adult is capable of communicating. Perhaps bigger than our society is ready to see or comprehend.

I hope you enjoy this book. It is your story. In a sense it is every girl's story. I hope you see yourself somewhere in these pages and feel reassured that, in this world, you are not alone.

Kate Engelbrecht

What adjectives best describe you?

FUNNY, SARCASTIC, ARTISTIC, FUN STRONG

Wallflower, quite, artistic, shy, caring.

Bubbly & calm & optimistic Conscientious

Creative smart, shy, passionate, honest   outgoing, social, curious

Quiet, Colorful, Loving, creative.

Unique, independent, intelligent, compassionate, loving, and hard-working.

compassionate, sleepy, and doubtful   Benevolent, I guess.   Difficult.

(according to my mother) sparkly   musical, creative, different, unique, lyrical, Shy, loud, nice,   CREATIVE

Short, Unbroken, Unique, Weird.

confusing, rambuctious, reflecting, crazy

Compassionate, Vivacious, Bold, Curious

People say I'm creative, passionate, smart, caring, etc.

artsy, random, quiet, outgoing   Hard working, organized, loyal

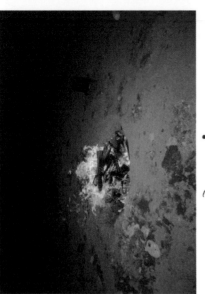

Quirky, independent, friendly   Creative
                                    Inquisitive

Outgoing, creative, compassionate

Unique, independent, diverse, artsy, eclectic

Dreamer, listener, (spelling nerd) short.

Strange, beautiful, young, Indie, New (Free, Lover, Dreamer
        Futuristic, Super cool) Stylish.

Funny, carefree, nerdy, different, cool, fun, adventurous, sporty, sweet,
                                                        understanding,
                                                        optimistic.
Prolific, Eccentric, Creative, reserved

Short, spunky, colorful and artsy.   (I hope....)

gutsy, adventurous, friendly, spontaneous

fun, random, loving, crazy, caring, creative, unique

Spaztic/friendly/Nice

22

Happy, cheerful, small yet adorable, smart, strong, awesome

confused, loving, teasing, loud, shy, self-conscious

radical, idealistic, intellectual, philosophical, conscientious, dynamic, impressionable

Serious, Funny, Positive, Weird.

Silly, dorky, thoughtful, always laughing, creative

fun shy smart interesting creative

Calm, Collected, responsible, patient, open-minded, thinker

PUNK, MUSICAL, Random, Accepting, kind, open minded

amazing outgoing, emotional, energetic, sympathetic, impatient

happy, Funny, creative, shy, confident, smart, driven

Foolish, silly, intelligent, caring, shy, outgoing, trickey, tall, wide, happy, hard-to-find, sensitive and beautiful.

Being me involves understanding that fitting in is not an option or I'd be lying to myself. I'm different, I'm awkward and opinionated and tend to say what I feel but that's ok. The best people in this world are a little out there so I'm in good company.

I push for everyone to be counted as equals. I have amazing people around me everyday and I usually fall asleep with a smile on my face.

I see beautiful things everywhere.

I'm different.

People, I look good in guys' clothes. I won't apologize for that. Stop being jealous because I have great style. Let me be!

I never really felt like I was connected with teenage girls I am very socially awkward and never really learned how to just "hangout" with other girls my age. I'm working on learning.

I dont really know who I am yet or what I want to do w/ my life and that worries me.

Answering the following questions is not required to participate in The Girl Project, though I would really appreciate your comments. Be as specific as you like. Send in with your camera and release form. Your name is not on this piece of paper and will not be used in conjunction with your identity.

1.) What adjectives best describe you?
random, fun, sincere, dramatic, free-spirited, artsy, fabulous, theatrical, outlandish, obnoxious, kind-hearted.

2.) What is the hardest part about being a teenager?
Sometimes we try to grow up too fast, and with all of the pressures of getting a boyfriend and getting good grades, life seems pretty difficult some times. Also, hormones kind of suck a lot. :)

3.) What is the best part about being a teenager?
There are so many things I can get away with (especially in regards to how I dress/act) that I most definitely couldn't if I was older or younger.

4.) What are your favorite qualities in a person?
Honesty, humor, being serious when need be, encouraging, fun, don't try to change you

5.) What is your idea of happiness?
Not caring what others think, and being true to YOURSELF. Also, skittles; they're pretty awesome, too. :)

6.) What is your ideal profession?
Fashion or Costume designer

7.) Tell me one thing about you that nobody else seems to get?
That just because I like rainbows and I'm a gay rights activist, it doesn't mean I'm a lesbian.

8.) What is your favorite color? Rainbow Sparkly (which is definitely a color)" [or blue]

9.) If you could live anywhere in the world, where would you live?
New York City, for sure.

10.) What do you think about the way(s) that teenage girls are portrayed in our culture? I think that a lot of people seem to shove us into different labels and categories because of how we dress or look or act. Just because someone has blonde hair or likes the color pink does not make them a barbie, or because someone dresses in all black doesn't make them "goth" or emo. There is too much strong place for people who conforming to labels, even for people who fitting in and fears itself. don't dress "normally."

11.) What are you afraid of?
Spiders, rejection, and fears itself.

12.) What are you most proud of?
That I dress the way I want to, not the way others want me to. And I feel comfortable with myself, no matter If I'm wearing a dress and combat boots or sweat pants.

14.) In as many or few words necessary, tell me about being you.
Mostly, I am defined by my love of all things sparkly. And cute. And rainbow. And happy. And sometimes sad. And DIY. And magic markers. And Nylon magazine. And vintage clothes/jewelry. And Betsey Johnson. And John Galliano. And olives. (The Sixas. And getting mail from Pen Pals. And making Fields. and Reading. And PJ Pants. And vanilla icecream topped with honey and rainbow sprinkles. And my cat. And metallic lunch boxes. And my hair (which is Pink). And cheap clothes from thrift stores. And roller skates. And bubble gum. And lollipops. And being myself no matter what.

More people need to give me a chance.

Being me is hard. I try to accept anyone into my life whom has been rejected by others.

I hide myself away with smiles and juicy gossip. I am not happy, at all.

I hate being me. I am never skinny enough or pretty enough. I tell myself I will never let the kids at school see me cry; because then they win.

I'm a very complicated person.

It's hard being me. I'm a bisexual living in a small, midwestern town. No one understands what I go through at home.

I am a soul-full passionate girl that can't stand
when people love to hate, I will talk to everyone because
I beleive that everyone deserves a friend no matter how different
however quiet they may seem, I'm a lover not a hater!!

It's hard being me, but really, it's just hard being a
teenage girl. My life to outsides would seem pretty
good but in my head its much worse. My life isn't
that bad, I guess I'm ~~some~~ exagerating a little. I have
friends and family that care a bout me but how far will
that take me when I don't feel very good a bout myself?
What good will acceptance do when I can't accept who I am?

44

many places as I can,

I desperitly want to see the world and travel as

I like girls. I find them attractive and funny and sexy.
This doesn't mean that my soul is damned.

I'm a good friend. I'm complex.
I'm naïve. I like to be silly. I
don't like the way I look. I'm a
follower, not a leader. Music and
photography are my outlets.
People don't remember me, but
they don't forget me either.

I blush way too much, and get embarrassed when
I'm the center of attention even at age 17. Lays
still make me nervous.

I'm strong and very intelligent. I know who I am, and
I know I need help becoming an adult. I'm 5'2 and 110 lbs
with 00 gauges in my ears and a lip ring. I really don't
fit any stereotype and I'm friends with everyone. I
have an obsessted with love.

pictures are easier to describe me
than words are. my camera is
my eye my eye that sees thing
that i don't.

Tell me one thing about you that nobody else seems to get.

why I am the way I am. Sometimes I just want to be alone

I have no real sense of time. I value relationships over punctuality. If a friend of mine was having personal issues during class, I would skip my class to comfort them. I enjoy everything I do and I don't see the point in being rushed. I'm tougher than I look. Seriously.   I just want to feel loved.

I love the wrong people and hurt the people that love me...   Why I like bats so much, they're just cool.

I want to get out of my hometown!   People don't get my preference of records.
I want to be accomplished at the professional level.   only mp3's or cd's
I want to climb mountains, tour cities - LIVE!

I accept leaving people behind, and have no   I make light of difficult situations.
problem picking up and leaving - it's what moving as   I'm in a great place now, but I've
                                    a child does to you... been emotionally beaten & scared.

I want to get a tatoo because it means   how strong my feelings are sometimes.
something and my family doesn't care for it.   or maybe how I see the world.

Trying to break the image people have for me.   I love to have a good time, but there is a time and a place.
I'm not about looks, I love personalities.   Disrespect to others is one of my biggest pet peeves.

        I'm really a fun person. Sadly, I'm super type-A and most only
        see me in strict situations.

that my belief system is allowed to be mine and does not
need to follow anyone else's.

I like to be alone sometimes, & just sit & think. Most
people find it bothersome, but I enjoy it.

How I find beauty in the small things and the little strange things I understand more than people think I do... At least I think so.

that I have extremely low self esteem

I don't think anyone will ever understand my emotions all the way. It sounds strange, but sometimes I think I fall in love with the most simplest of things too easily, which crushes me just as easy.

How hyper I am, or that I have a voice

My mind

I love Japan.

I'm a teenage republican, don't find many of those around

I don't wear shoes to represent peace.

My sense of spirituality and my thoughts on religion,

I'm not a people person. It continues on till I become blind numb, even before I meet them. I find quirks that loops long time, and do my thing I keep myself to get together.

Why I care about people so much or how sensitive I really am to criticism or how many things actually are for me.

I am not like most teens. I don't find material things. I am happy with what I have and don't use bad words.

Although I work out a lot I feel healthy and am secure with I'm toned. I still struggle with eating (body issues)

I do things I say too much out of spite & on a whim. I used to keep everything bottled up as a kid so now I just say what I do whatever's on my mind. It gets me in trouble.

that it's okay to be friends **I believe I'm more experienced +**
with people in other cliques **intelligent than people understand.**

I am content with spending my saturday night
at the bookstore reading & drinking coffee all by myself
and I love it.

why im always happy despite the circumstances.

No one seems to get me somehow when I feel like crying, I smile
I am hyper, or just the overall way that I see things. - I actually AM overweight and people need to stop telling me
otherwise.

I'm always happy and on the good side, people don't
get that I'm simply happy

I can see in the raysen a creepy child so weird ways

I really am aware of things... "I KNOW!" stop acting like I'm oblivious!

I never really felt like I was connected with teenage girls I am very socially awkward
and never really learned how to just "hangout" with other girls my age. I'm working on learning.

That I'm not really that good a person that they think I
am. At school, I pretend to be a nice, good person. But I have a
dark side that only my boyfriend knows.

That just because I like rainbows and I'm a gay rights
activist, it doesn't mean I'm a lesbian.

I GIVE OFF AN AIR OF NONCHALANCE ABOUT THINGS,
BUT I PROBABLY DO CARE A LOT

I hate chocolate but I love hot chocolate.

I think I've reached such a state of conciousness that I see
past friendships/relationships and it scares me.

That through the years I've learned, that im muchmore mature and wiser. That "y dont know how the real world is".

I dont intend to come off as aloof or standoffish

I can do anything I put my mind to. Telling me I cant only brings me down.

struggle to speak up & stand up for what I want

I try really hard to make everyone happy around me

- Nobody seems to get why I'm so open with my feelings. I'm definitely an open book and I'm not afraid to show my emotions, opinions, etc... with strangers.

My love for art and people turn the world.

I have a lot of guy friends and naturally get along with guys, but a lot of girls I meet think I flirt endlessly and like every guy I talk to. I just like talking to people and making lots of friends!!

nobody understands how I can keep a secret or promise. I know so many secrets that my friends have told me. my family has told me, and no one understands what allows me to keep them all. little do they know how many of my own secrets I have...

I'm not like everyone else in the sense somewhere than I have
in. I have different interests, attitudes, beliefs, and orientations
that make me feel isolated where I live.

I am a quiet person. Its just... no one sees that side of me,
because I am a little louder when I'm with my friends. So when I
read my horoscope, and my laugh at how "wrong" it is, it makes me sad.

I don't want to be wrong!

Me being serious, because to them I'm always the
laidback, funny one.

I'm not really what you would call "religious"
I worship God in my own way.

I feel I'm more mature than
everyone else so I don't find the crude
jone's funny.

When I had sex I didn't "lose"
anything, rather, I gained something.

That I am a completely different person
when I am alone

Why I care more about my FUTURE than
other.

I just like to think sometimes...

I just want to turn to be held. Loved for who I am. Listened to.

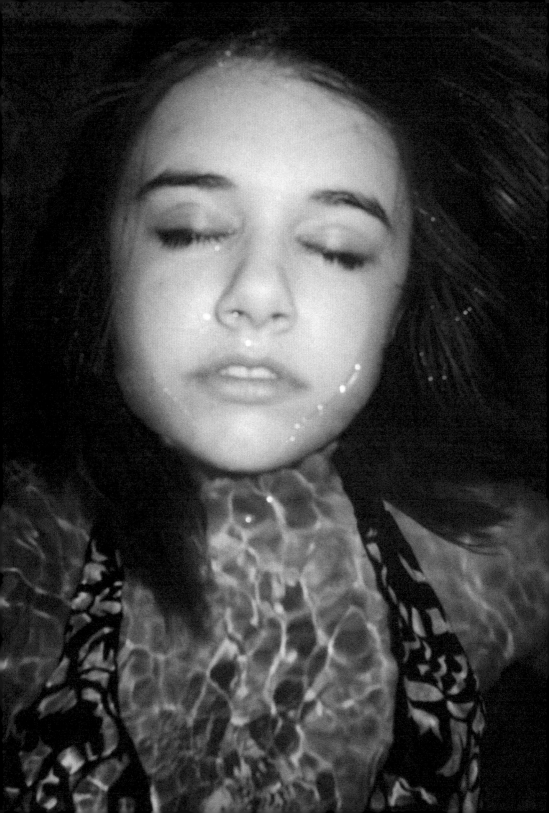

i love people. i love learning about different cultures and languages. this is why i want to travel. i want to go and see and learn new things. i love animals. at the moment, i have snakes, cats, a dog, a crested gecko, and a tarantula. i would love to see other animals around the world. i also love art. i really do believe it's everywhere. it's in all these things i just mentioned. i love to see it and i love to make it. my room is covered in drawings, stickers, magazine pictures. i like to draw and paint. i like painting my body, especially if it glows in my black light. i like to experiment with make-up & paint my sister's face. and i love photography. these things are part of my life and they make me happy.

i like to do what makes me happy and believe in what i believe in. i don't do things other teens do. i try hard. and strive for perfection. i have big dreams and i will reach them.

Answering the following questions is not required to participate in The Girl
Project, though I would really appreciate your comments. Be as specific as you
like. Send in with your camera and release form. Your name is not on this piece of
paper and will not be used in conjunction with your identity.

1.) What adjectives best describe you?

Short, Unbroken, Unique, Weird.

2.) What is the hardest part about being a teenager?

not ~~knowing~~ following after the World

3.) What is the best part about being a teenager?

living you life, being your hearts desire

4.) What are your favorite qualities in a person?

has a heart full of Jesos Christ

5.) What is your idea of happiness?

JESUS,

6.) What is your ideal profession?

Welling, Photography

7.) Tell me one thing about you that nobody else seems to get?

I dont wear Shoes To represent Peace.

8.) What is your favorite color? red

9.) If you could live anywhere in the world, where would you live?

Canada or England

10.) What do you think about the way(s) that teenage girls are portrayed in our culture? I think it is awfull, girls are gods creation, no one is the same. We are beautiful in our sun ways.

11.) What are you afraid of?

Homeless People, falling into the world

12.) What are you most proud of?

The life that god has brought into my hands.

14.) In as many or few words necessary, tell me about being you.

Tomboy, Vegetarian, Skateboarder, Photographer, JesusFreak, nothing can bring me down.

Answering the following questions is not required to participate in The Girl Project, though I would really appreciate your comments. Be as specific as you like. Send in with your camera and release form. Your name is not on this piece of paper and will not be used in conjunction with your identity.

1.) What adjectives best describe you?

Humorous / Conceited / Fun / Spontaneous / Artistically talented

2.) What is the hardest part about being a teenager?

The transition from Adolescence to Adulthood. Reality sets in when you realize that your dreams will be extremely difficult to acheive.

3.) What is the best part about being a teenager?

My social life and the outrageous events that follow.

4.) What are your favorite qualities in a person?

Sense of humor / Optimism / Sense of Style / Intelligence

5.) What is your idea of happiness?

For my Artistic talent and Creativity to take me far.

6.) What is your ideal profession?

Something that creatively challenges me without boring me,

7.) Tell me one thing about you that nobody else seems to get?

The fact that I truely don't give a flying fuck about people's negative views on me.

8.) What is your favorite color? Black and every shade of grey.

9.) If you could live anywhere in the world, where would you live?
New York City, I'm so sick of Peoria.

10.) What do you think about the way(s) that teenage girls are portrayed in our culture? As with every stereotype, there is a deeper layer conviently avoided by the eyes of the public masses. I don't appreciate the fact that teenage girls tend to be classified so readily with ignorant perceptions. But then again, don't mes↑

11.) What are you afraid of?
Hate crimes against my sexual orientation. It's happened before, and is not pleasant. And... ignorant People.

12.) What are you most proud of?
My artwork. Getting A's on my art in my college courses.

14.) In as many or few words necessary, tell me about being you.
I have never "belonged" in a stereotype. I am not afraid to break the mold and stand above others with my confidence. I don't need anyone's approval to be comfortable in my own skin. I know who I am. I know where I stand. It's your own loss if you instantly judge me and miss out on a pretty great friendship. :)
To me, being free spirited is the perfect way to enjoy life.

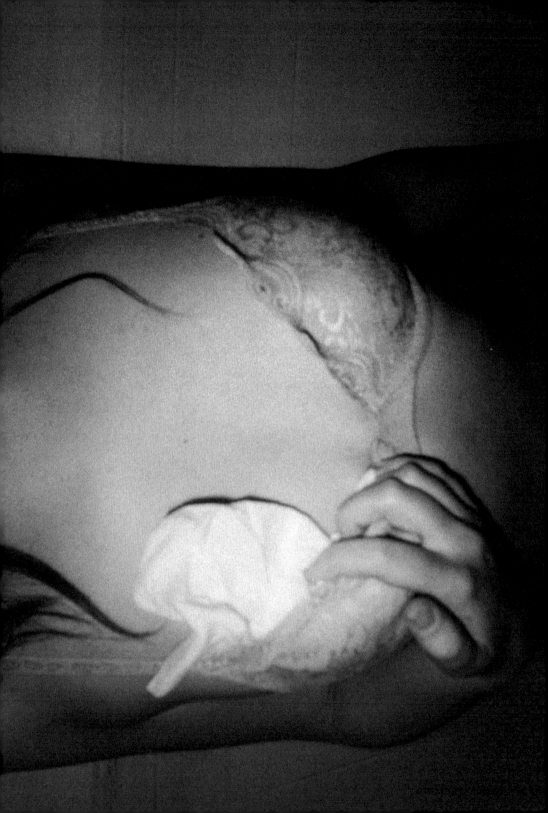

I think the hardest thing that all teenagers go through is figuring out Not knowing who you're going to be. who you are, what you believe in, and your purpose in life.

The constant mood swings and the want to rebel against any and all authority.

Being on the journey to self-discovery while being scrutinized from every angle.

The hardest part about being a teenager is over-coming differences. I think teenagers face racial differences and personality differences and have to overcome them to make friends and grow.

people do not understand what you are really feeling because our parents grew up in a different decade.

Being on the journey to self-discovery while being scrutinized from every angle.

Everything? I dont know, everything is stressful and hormones and its just chaotic you wonder it is all even worth it in the end.

Dealing with the stress of school, home, and relationships.

It is really hard trying to find a balance between school, a social life, and other after school activities.

You are unable t make decisions on your own and there are so many pressures from your parents, peers, teachers and yourself.

Probably trying to find myself; trying to establish what kind of person I want to be... Also, boys are a path to deal with!

I would say the hardest part about being a teenager is knowing that being an adult comes next.

Wanting more out of life than opportunity allows. Finding that place that you fit in in this world Being Restricted or held back

meeting expectations held by parents, friends, teachers (as cliche as it sounds) establishing your own identity

Learning everything through making mistakes and getting hurt.

High school for sure, it's a big problem-filled with little good things.

trying to decide what is socially acceptable socially acceptable know what im doing "and i'll learn" or "I told you so" took me a LonG time "your too young to know what love is" or to understand this

because I am young and just a teenager nobody thinks I

So much stress, and dealing with the stereotypical teens.

People saying to be like myself or whatever were everyone is. If they're be like me, and so I'm a bit of dumb of silly (lame, how totaled with people who continually face discrimination once again.)

People tend to think you're stupid because you don't know the way the life.

meeting expectations held by parents, friends, teachers (as cliche as it sounds)

establishing your own identity

I think being unique/yourself is hard, because all you want in jr. high and maybe in high school is to have friends and so you buy a mini skirt and a polo shirt and say you like Britney Spears because no one length skirts and Nirvana just don't cut it.

experience to back up your beliefs.

probably peer pressure and the fact that my parents are going through a divorce

I think it would be managing time, and realizing that being a teenager is really just that step before becoming an adult

peer pressure and the fact that my parents are going through a divorce

Being stuck between the age of innocence and no freedom, and the age of total freedom. I mean, I only get a taste of what freedom is, and it's limited.. My parents remind me daily that at among 13.

being so confused about everything. there are so many new things to think about and comprehend

people not considering my opinions or arguments valid because I am younger than them and they think I'm a teen I don't back my argument up with research, which I do.

I believe life in general is hard, but the teenage years are when we experience & learn. It's difficult from what to wear to weight, body image I believe is hardest for me.

The hardest part is all the drama we have to deal with on top of schoolwork.

Trying to be the girl that everyone expects you to be

82

not ~~always~~ following after the world

Keeping up with everything that's expected of you while still maintaining **Social norms, peer pressure** a strong sense of identity

I think the hardest part about being a teenager is not only living up to the expectations people make for you, but also live up to your own. There are so many people to please that it gets exhausting.
I believe that temptation is one of the hardest part of being a teenager.
Temptation could be anything. Sexual temptation, temptation to party had an scandal, and temptation to try things that could harm us.

Dealing with an unknown future and trying to deal with the things that come with growing up. It is also hard to accept that you have to be an adult some day and takecare of everything yourself soon.

Trying to do everything at one and excelling it/living up to high standards

the people + the emotional problems

Society's standards of beauty;
(and not being able to get into "R" rated movies... that sucks too)

Having people be extremely dependant on you & peer pressure (although I'm good at saying **NO**)

The hardest part is dealing with body issues. Loving yourself, being content with who you are. Not living up to the number on the scale. Dealing with rude, dumb comments & finding no privacy.

Trying to fit into a status quo that is impossible to achieve.

Having that content the struggle to prove yourself to achieve.

making your parents proud and appreciate you.

thinking about & what I want to do in life, fitting in but and the fear that I won't accomplish my goals also standing out at the same time

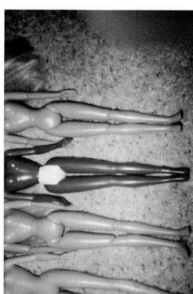

not being able to ~~say~~ say what you want or — Trying to get your parents trust.
express how you feel without getting in trouble

I think the hardest part is just finding someone you can   Having to prove to adults that we're not
trust and confide my feelings to. Sneaking out is actually
really hard too.   as immature, bad, dangerous, or dumb as they think.

every day   Over weight   Not having 100% creative
holds the unknown.   Freedom due to school+time restraints+teenage
                                                                awkwardness.

Scheduling fun in between school and work. We
all think we're adults and can handle it, but
we're not.

Identity! Sometimes I'm not sure if I should be who
I am, or who I'm "supposed" to be; or even who I want to be!

Fitting in and sometimes apperance.

        because I am young and just a teenager nobody thinks I
        know what I'm doing ("and I'll learn" or "I told you so") OR
        "Your too young to know what love is."

Sometimes we try to grow up too fast, and with all of the pressures
of getting a boyfriend and getting good grades, life seems pretty difficult some
times. Also, hormones kind of suck a lot. :)

I can't stick it in a bottle and save it.   The Limits People Put On You — @ Like Being Too Young,
                                            Too Inexperienced, Too Reckless

I'm always getting in trouble, so I'm grounded a lot.
And most of my friends hate me for getting a boyfriend, so
my life is kind of hard. :(

Answering the following questions is not required to participate in The Girl
Project, though I would really appreciate your comments. Be as specific as you
like. Send in with your camera and release form. Your name is not on this piece of
paper and will not be used in conjunction with your identity.

1.) What adjectives best describe you?
curvy, intelligent, quiet, thoughtful, honest, loyal, strong

2.) What is the hardest part about being a teenager?
The pressure. To be thin, beautiful, popular. To go to parties
and do drugs and drink and hook up with a random guy in
hopes of being cool. I won't do any of that. But it's hard.

3.) What is the best part about being a teenager?
I can't think of anything. I hate being a teenager.

4.) What are your favorite qualities in a person?
• Truthfulness
• sense of humor
• loyalty

5.) What is your idea of happiness?
No worries or stress; having the perfect body and being
beautiful; marrying an amazing guy who loves me for
who I am

6.) What is your ideal profession?
A photographer for the Denver Broncos

7.) Tell me one thing about you that nobody else seems to get?
I just want to feel loved.

8.) What is your favorite color? Hot Pink!

9.) If you could live anywhere in the world, where would you live?
Scotland.

10.) What do you think about the way(s) that teenage girls are portrayed in
our culture? It affects me so much even though I don't
tell anybody that. I hate it. I wish it would change
but it won't. It makes me hate myself.

11.) What are you afraid of?
• Never getting married and being alone forever because I'm
not good enough   • the dark   • being kidnapped & tortured
• spiders

12.) What are you most proud of?
My resistance to peer pressure

(continued on back)

13.) In as many or few words necessary, tell me about being you. I hate being me. I am never skinny enough or pretty
enough. I tell myself I will never let the kids at school see me cry;
because then they win. I love with all my heart yet I have never
had the chance to show somebody that. I am very empathetic. I
hide behind makeup. I cry but never in front of people. I will always
stand up for what I believe is right, regardless of whether or not
people disagree. I don't ever trust ANYONE. They just end up hurting you.
I am quiet a lot but always paying attention and I pick up on things
many people don't notice. Sometimes I feel like the weight of the world
is on my shoulders. I try to appear confident to the world but I'm not.

3) I wish I could fast-forward to a better time in life. Sometimes I tell friends I am busy and can't hang out, but really it's because I don't have money. I hate when people feel sorry for me. If I could trade lives with somebody beautiful I would love to do it just for a day, so I could know what it feels like. I love watching movies and reading books because they allow me to get lost and leave this world and all my problems, at least for a little while. I can't live without music; sometimes I feel like it's the only thing that keeps me going. I always look for shooting stars to make a wish on. I've tried throwing up after I eat and I've tried not eating at all, but I guess I just don't have what it takes to be beautiful. At times I am happy but then I remember everything that's wrong in my life and I come back to reality. I love photography because I'm not in the picture. I feel like I can write what I feel a lot better than I can actually say it. I wish I was really good at something, like a sport. I play volleyball but I am only average at it. I wish I could get my tear ducts removed. I hate crying. Crying = weakness. The one thing I love about myself are my eyes, people always think I'm wearing fake eyelashes, but I'm not. I want to move to Scotland because anywhere is better than here. Sometimes all I want is somebody who I can hug and don't ever need to let go. And who doesn't want to let go of me either. But I'm starting to think that will never happen. I love snow storms and thunder and lightning storms, I don't mind being alone because then there is nobody to judge me. I love football and I know a lot about it, which comes as a surprise to some people. All my female teachers never really like me for some reason. I have a penny collection. I hate summer because it means shorts and bathing suits, which everyone looks good in except me. I love my cat because he loves me no matter what. I didn't plan on writing this much but here you have it. My heart and soul are on this piece of paper. Things I've never told anyone. Use it as you will.

♡ Me

I'm a dreamer, I'm a thinker, I want to go places, and see the world.

What is the best part about being a teenager?

You get some freedom

Friendship and laughter :))

everyday holds the unknown.   no responsibility!

not too old and not too young.

Laugh, Love, Friendship, learning.

You can do better things in your life

As a teenager, the world is almost waiting for your teenage act of penance or voicing your opinion - I like finding ways to prove them right without being too arrogant or predictable.

THE LIMITS PEOPLE PUT ON YOU - @ LIKE BEING TOO YOUNG, TOO INEXPERIENCED, TOO RECKLESS

Boys & friends

Not having 100% creative
Freedom due to school, time restraints + teenage awkwardness.

Discovering who you're going to be @

The freedom of some adult responsibilities.

like I said, no job, no bills, and for the most part, I can do anything I like.

We're at the age where we are learning; exploring.
The age of Exploration. we become passionate for various things. we begin to learn the true meaning of life.

freedom. ability to hope for the future.

Discovering yourself

You can explore... make some stupid choices without all of the consequences and then learn from your mistakes.

being with friends, meeting new people, taking risks + trying new things.

What is the best part about being a teenager?

The fact that we aren't adults but still get some responsibility and they slack some of the rules

We sometimes enjoyed freedom of a time before "real" life as they call it begins

The best part of being a teenager is being coddled by your parents you don't have a worry in the world.

There are so many things I can get away with (especially in regards to how I dress/act) that I most definitely couldn't if I was older or younger.

- being old enough to roam alone, but too young to be self-sufficient

Hanging out with friends and finding out who we are and what we want to do in life.

being myself & accepting my surroundings

Being old enough to make big choices, but young enough that it's still ok to make mistakes.

Learning as we mature. Growing as a human.

Being able to have your life ahead of you and being able to still act like a kid sometimes and not have people look at you funny.

Not having to ~~taxes~~ worry or pay taxes

Being happy & feeling free & experiencing new things

Being able to need a job, free responsibility. I don't pay the bills.

Not having to worry, having no real cares, when there's a lack of parents, getting kicked out, longboarding at 3am, walking everywhere, being broke, pretend we're 18, laughing at this, getting lost, allnighters, talkin my girls while laughing until we cry

The best part about being a teenager is having experiences. Experiencing firsts, love, heartbreak, freedom, responsibility, driving, and searching for jobs and colleges.

Discovering who you're going to be &

Being able to mess up and know you can fall back on someone. Having opportunities and free time. Learning to deal

I don't pay rent, insurance, I can't

The fact that it's the best years of your life you don't have to worry life carefree at this time.

The best part about being a teenager is the feeling of finding starting to know yourself its the time where you make your own opinions up, and people actually begin to listen.

Being able to live through life without worrying so much because your parents got your back and your friends are always there

having your needs, such as food and shelter, fulfilled for free

Just learning about life and myself.

having the opportunities to express myself and find out who I am as a person

All the spontaneous moments. For example going to the movies and then driving to the super store to run around & push your friends in shopping carts.

experimenting with different styles + activities + having the freedom to decide your likes & dislikes for yourself

Having the time of your life!

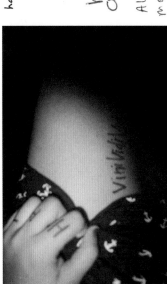

Virility

It's like ~~xxxxxx~~ said in "the Perks of being a wallflower" ...something about feeling infinite. That's the best part.

Being trusted. Having a cell phone, because my parents know I won't run up the phone bill. Or maybe the wide variety of people you can meet when you're a teenager?

The best part about being a teenager is how you get to feel and experience the world in such a passionate way that only teens can.

having good relationships and best friends and making new friends. also just being young and enjoying life!

The best part is surpassing people's expectations

Feeling as if you can truly do anything with your life.

The best part would have to be the freedom we are gaining and the fun we get to have.
Being able to live life and make mistakes but to know someone is there to fix it.

Becoming the adult I want to be.

No responsibilities - no bills, no mortgage. I can just have fun, go to the Playground for days on end. Chill at the mall, go to camp. I am expressing myself and around up and into Someone I'm glad to be.

Having an excuse to be irresponsible, and the fact that its okay make mistakes

Going out to places, hanging out with friends

being **FREE** & careless

being young and having fun to build yourself as a person and have adventures and figure out who you are.

The best part about being a teenager is having fun with friends. My best memories have been with my friends and it's those memories that I'll remember my teen years by.

I can't think of anything, I hate being a teenager. Having the ability to make horrible mistakes and have it blamed on being young.

the crazy adventures with friends complete with wild antics that are completely acceptable, because your "just being a teenager"

The new awareness that we have as we get older that says, "Hey! You're an adult now - well almost.

Being treated like an adult but still being stupid like a child sometimes being between adulthood and childhood isn't so bad. And knowing more about the world.

Being able to discover yourself and gain some freedoms before you are completely immersed in adulthood.

It's the perfect in between being a child and an adult.

living your life, being your hearts desire

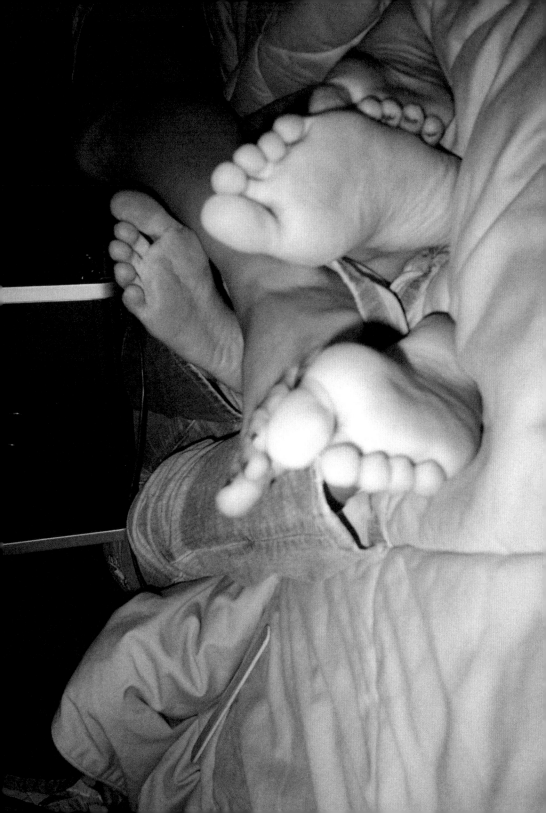

What is your ideal profession?

shooting film for fashion designers, magazines.

an illustrator working alongside Allen Moore

artist.

librarian Writer, social worker Photographer. Artist

nurse.

I want to animate films. doctor of physical therapy

translator for the United Nations

artist. lawyer part-time photographer

sociologist. photographer

stay at home mom!

psychologist

Graphic Design Artist

painter

a psychologist+ Design.

PROFESSIONAL PHOTOGRAPHER

photographer/environmentalist

writer

create clothing. Art

A photographer for the Denver Broncos

travelling photographer

To create short films and products that make people happy.

writing   music supervisor   Photographer

Photographer   fashion designer

A journalist or novelist;
anything that can help me show a picture/idea.

musician   Photography   A lawyer   Photography

Fashion or Costume designer   graphic designer

Artist   **Singer**   photographer   Artist.

Doctor   **photojournalist,**

World-traveling Freelance photographer

Chef   Ideal: a writer

musician   Anything involving music.

interior designer   Photographer

Chef / RESTAURANT OWNER

HAIR COLORIST

Photographer

fashion psychologist fashion designer.

Photographer, pilates teacher

actress PHOTOGRAPHY

anything that allows me to run wild!

Teaching

veterinarian A cake decorator

dermatologist Photographer.

pastry chef? a journalist or book editor

make a difference.

doctor zoo keeper fashion model ?

Photographer♥ Welling art fashion design

fashion designer maybe? lawyer in either business or entertainment

CinemaMakeup art photographer

teacher

photographer, FBI or In CIA

National Geographic Photography   Humanitarian

orthodontist don't know yet

Photography or Film-   Doctor

Realisticly: a Psychologist

english teacher for inner city teens

photographer

Something related to history or political science.
Journalist   Likly, a professor.

A Photographer

mom   An actress

Photographer!

physiologist

a highschool art teacher

veternarian

Photographer   interior design

hydrologist. Photography Bradway Ster Photography

photographer/Photorrralist, PHOTOGRAPHER!!,

Neurosurgeon astrophysicist Egyptology teacher.

middle/high School English teacher. photographer environmental scientist

astronaut. Emergency Medical Technician Pre-school teacher

kindergarden teacher

Psycologist photographer

working with kids

artist nurse **Helping those in need.**

A National Geographic photojournalist

I want to write, I want to inspire, I want to enlighten, I want to give a voice to the oppressed. I have alot of energy + passion + can not wait to get out of here and use it!

I am strange, adventurous, I love music. I play bass. I have friends who got my back. I know nothing of what my future beholds. I love video games. I have a lot of guy friends. I'm feirce and stylish. I have an adopted brother who is actually my cousin. I am a painter. I wanna make films + bake cakes. I Dye my hair too much. I love hugs. I used to be addicted to self violence. I am a hopeless romantic Is ing too much. I don't smile. I Love him.

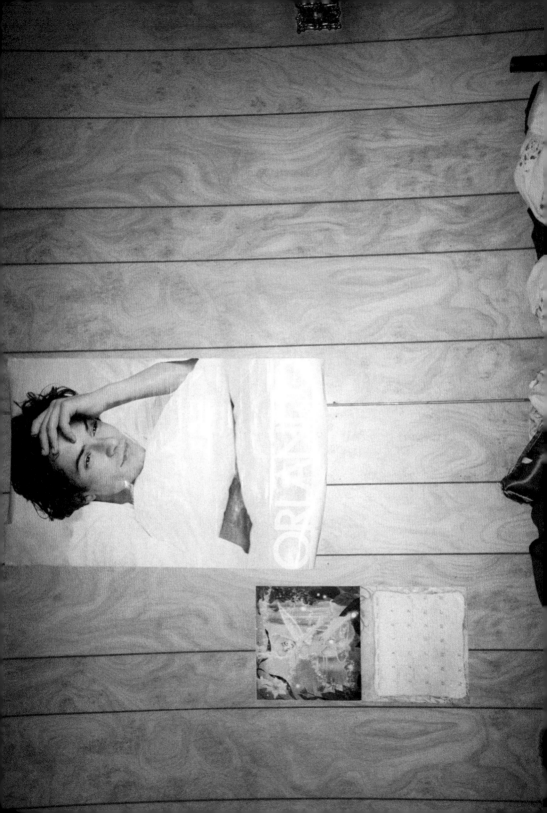

The Perfect Girl
by Fiona Eileen Campbell

We all know that girl.
We see her flawless body. We smell her expensive perfume, we hear
her tinkling laughter, and we touch her porcelain skin. Then we
taste the envy burning in the back of our throats.

She's perfect.

We all know her. We all know hundreds of girls like her.
But how well did we get to know them?

Did we assume that because they are beautiful and feminine,
they are ignorant and carefree? Did we assume that these
girls are mere copies of one another, incapable of
independent or intelligent thought?

Did we bother to get to know any one of these perfect girls? to know any one of these perfect girls?

This perfect girl hates the way she looks. She stares in the mirror, peering disdainfully at those glossy curls we would kill to have. She frowns at her beautiful, exotic features. She feels out of place and unhappy. Did we know that?

That perfect girl thinks she's too fat. She compares her attractive hourglass figure to those models in Vogue, and deems herself disgusting. She wonders if maybe she skipped a few meals a day she could lose some weight. Did we know that?

Another perfect girl is wracked with fear. Her charming, charismatic personality caused her to fall for a boy equally as wonderful, but she's too insecure to

to tell him. She stuffs her bra with kleenex, thinking that this will attract the attention she's looking for. Did we know that?

Did we know that one perfect girl is not the same as any other perfect girl?
Did we know that she's really not perfect?

We didn't even know that she was capable of thinking about anything other than what she's going to do Friday night.

But she is

She's worrying about our situation in Iraq. She's missing her mother who died a year ago, or her brother who just left for college. She's wondering how she'll manage to cope with three tests, a quiz, and a broken heart on top of all that. And yes, she's thinking about what she's going to do Friday night.

She houses the same emotions every girl does. Fear. Anxiety. Insecurity. Hope. Love. Life.

When we looked into her eyes, we got distracted by the mascara and forgot to look into her soul. But it's beautiful, and it is unique to the girl that she is. Not the movie stars perfect girl that others think she is, but her.

When asked, many will say that there are thousands of girls in the world. But they're wrong. There's one, and another, and another, and another....

Every girl feels with the strongest emotion, but there is a spectrum of feelings. Every girl lives

with the utmost animation, but there are so many motivations. Every girl strives with the highest passion, but there are so many things to be passionate about.

The perfect girl is forever elusive. She flits about our minds, hovers above our dreams, and dances through our deepest emotions (like the wind.

"Girl." The term describes all of us, and yet, it describes no one.

I am just a 14 year old girl trying
to lead a normal, happy life.

I live a really normal life. I don't party too much.
I just hang out with my closest friends and have
a good time. I love school and learning. I love reading
and swimming. I express myself through writing and
photography. I am religious. I love GOD.

I'm just me.

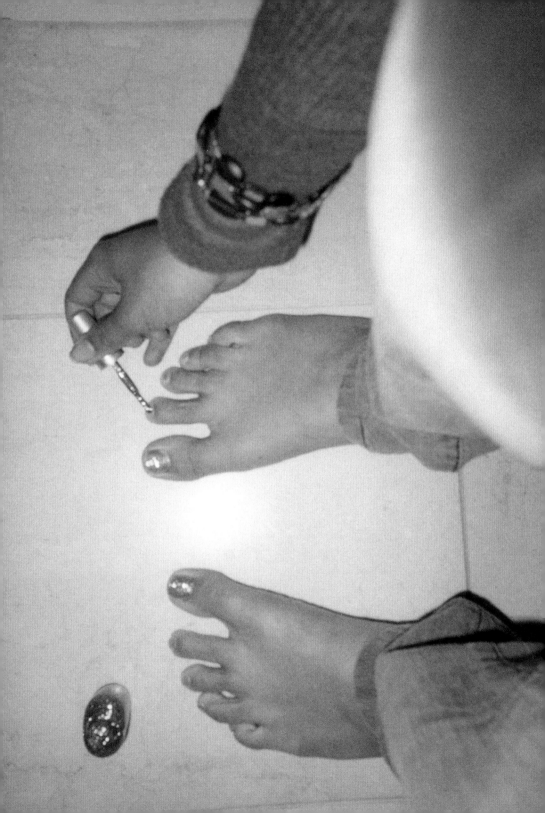

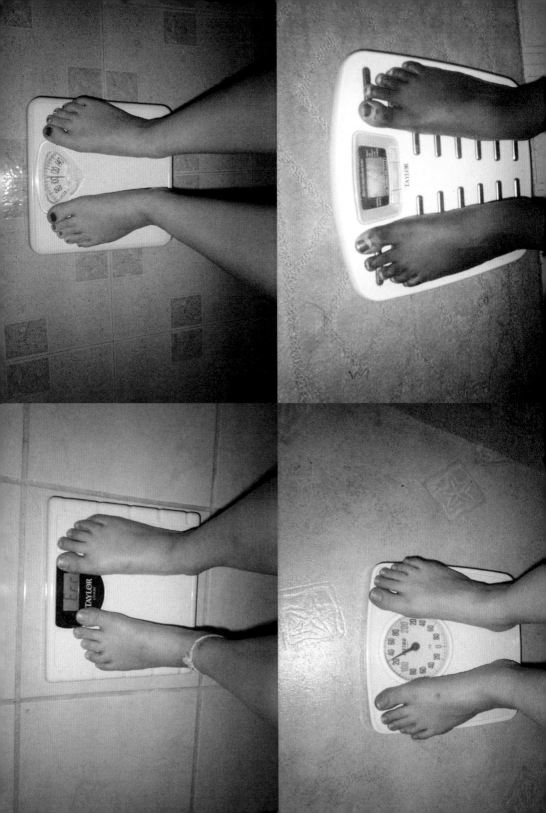

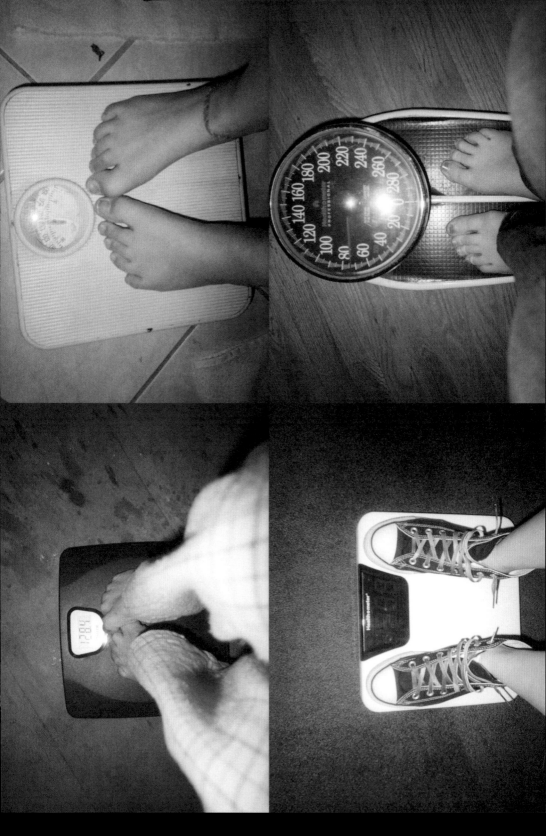

Answering the following questions is not required to participate in The Girl
Project, though I would really appreciate your comments. Be as specific as you
like. Send in with your camera and release form. Your name is not on this piece of
paper and will not be used in conjunction with your identity.

1.) What adjectives best describe you?
Foolish, silly, intelligent, caring, shy, outgoing, trickey, tall, wide,
happy, hard-to-find, sensitive and beautiful.

2.) What is the hardest part about being a teenager?
The hardest part is dealing with body issues. Loving yourself,
being content with who you are. Not caring about the number on
the scale. Dealing with rude, dumb comments & finding happiness.

3.) What is the best part about being a teenager?
Being able to mess up and know you can fall back on someone.
Having opportunities, and free time. Learning to deal,

4.) What are your favorite qualities in a person?
Honesty, patience, kind, excited, fun, daring, outgoing, loud, and
caring.

5.) What is your idea of happiness?
My idea of happiness is loving myself. Being content with
who I am, and my surroundings. Being care-free.

6.) What is your ideal profession?
I am not sure. I would love to work with the FBI or in CIA. But
I would also love to be a photographer, or a painter.

7.) Tell me one thing about you that nobody else seems to get?
No one seems to get my emotions. When I feel like crying, I cry.
I am hyper, or just the overall body that I see things.

8.) What is your favorite color? Black

9.) If you could live anywhere in the world, where would you live?
I would like to live in New York City.

10.) What do you think about the way(s) that teenage girls are portrayed in our culture? Our culture enjoys sterotyping girls. Society sees us as ignorant, and promiscuous. They make it seem like all we care about is how we look & gossip. I on the otherhand, actually think about my future and boys are the last thing on my mind. I am the least promiscuous

11.) What are you afraid of? Since I've never had a boyfriend. But I can't speak for all. I am afraid of becoming my mother. I am afraid of falling into a sterotype. I am scared of marriage, and clowns, and hospitals.

12.) What are you most proud of?
I don't think I am proud of anything... I guess I am proud of where my family has come, and about having a beautiful genious for a daughter but I have still yet to find what makes me proud.

14.) In as many or few words necessary, tell me about being you.
Being me is simple, but I make it hard. I get upset when I shouldn't, and think too hard about what is to come. But my life is usually boring with a few outburts or unexpected, exciting events. Being me isn't easy. It should be, but I guess I am too sensitive. Being me takes time, thought, and tears. (when it shouldn't.) Being me is ... a never ending story—

PRETTY IN P

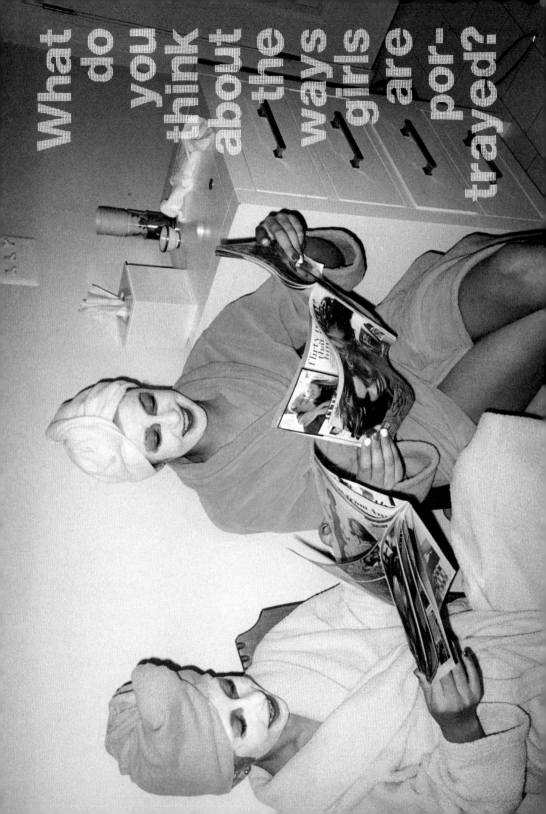

What do you think about the ways girls are por-trayed?

TEENAGE GIRLS ARE STILL OVERLOOKED - WOMEN ARE BEGINNING TO GET THERE DESERVED PLACE IN THE WORLD, BUT GIRLS STILL HAVE TROUBLE BEING HERRO AMONG OTHER TEENS AND ADULTS

I guess we're portrayed as skinny little whores who will do anything to be as thin as a twig.

I think that they are portrayed really badly. Not every teen girl would go have sex and get pregnant with some random dude.

I think its bullshit being a teenage girl is so much more than just sleepovers, make up and boys.

I think that our society tries to sculpt teenage girls 3 that we are seen through others ideas of what they want their image to be

I think its awful. The media is showing the human race how to live, and the females are getting the worst part of it.

skinny stupid whores obsessing over makeup, boys, and always saying they're fat to fish for compliments. Get Real.

i dislike it. I dislike the way girls are being pressured to be some sort of sex icon. Its crazy.

Honestly, we all seem to look "sleazy". It's very degrading to me, because I know we're better than that.

I think it's sad. Girls shouldn't have to weigh 100 pounds and have perfect skin and sleep with the whole football team to be accepted. Sure "attractive" People draw others to them naturally, but I think our definition of attractiveness is warped.

Teenage girls for the most part are painted as insecure and easily manipulated. For the most part, this isn't the case. I feel that the media focuses on the worst of our generation and do not often enough appreciate the great things about us.

I think they are oversexualized and idealized. The wrong ideals are encouraged,

148

teenage girls are unfairly rushed to become adults while they still want I hate the way we are portrayed in our culture to be children - the inappropriate ways they are shown sickens me

I think adults portray as they wish high school is like without I think teenage girls have to grow up to fast and think doing research. because of our popular culture. In the media, we all become sex icons, objects, butt-shaking, hair-waving, perfect

They think teens are careless and naive. We're just figuring out who we are as people.

Teenage girls are portrayed as sex symbols. There's so much pressure for a girl to be thin, pretty, popular...

People think that teenage girls only care about shopping, dieting and boys but most girls I know are actually enlightened and well adjusted.

Girls are portrayed as these little rays of sunshine that are happy about everything. either that or they portray them as being pregnant.

honestly, it's way too superficial and sexual the way girls are portrayed. guys our age think it's okay to sleep with lots of girls. and girls are going along with it. life shouldn't be revolving around that stuff. sex is for marriage. we should still be having fun as kids.

I think a lot of teen girls are thought of as sluts because they try too hard

They've got it all wrong. Every girl is different. There should not be any stereotype for teen girls ———> it steals their individuality.

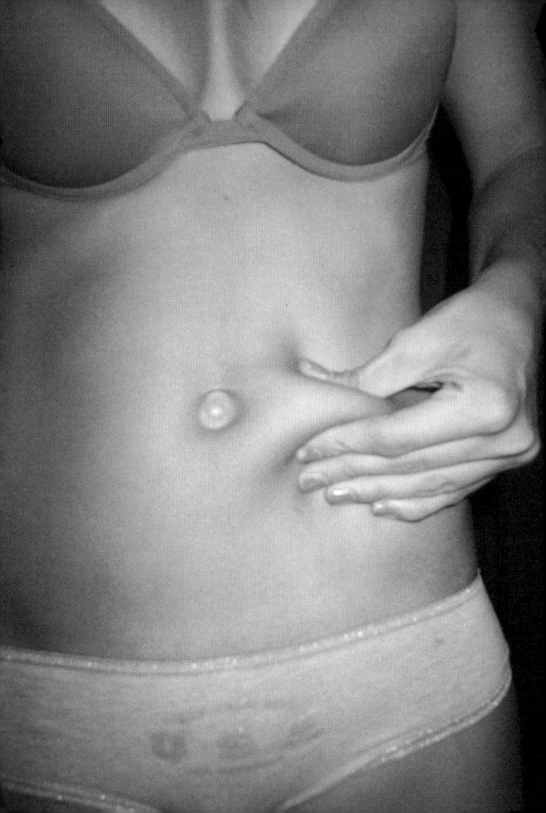

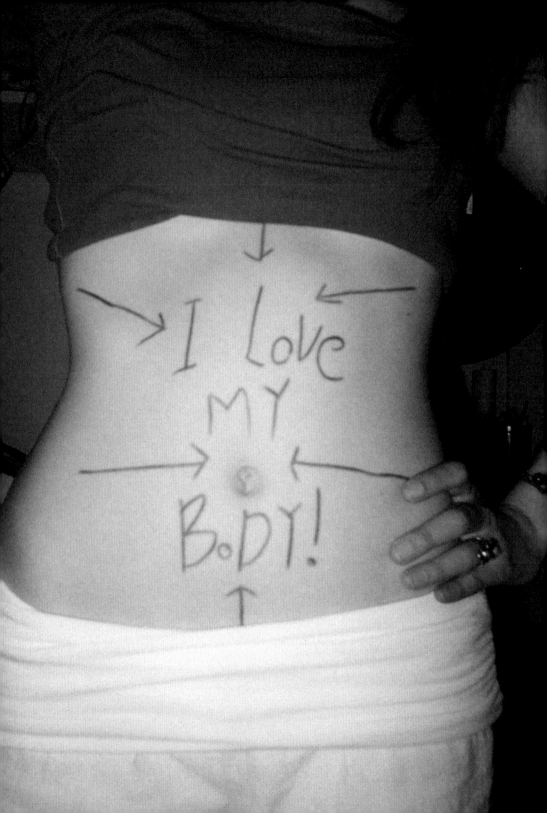

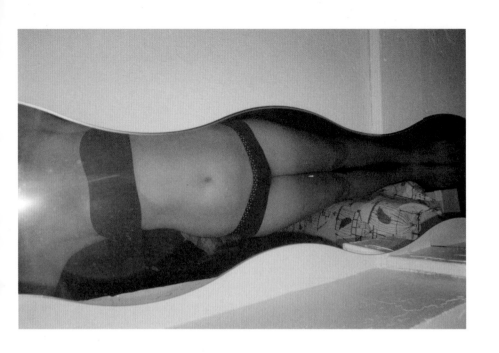

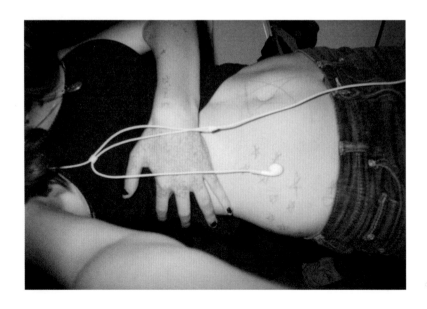

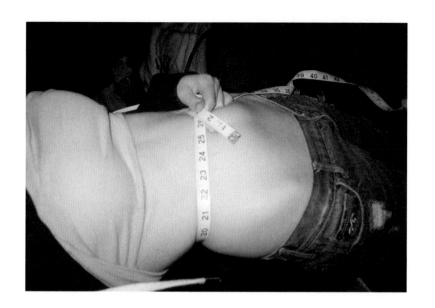

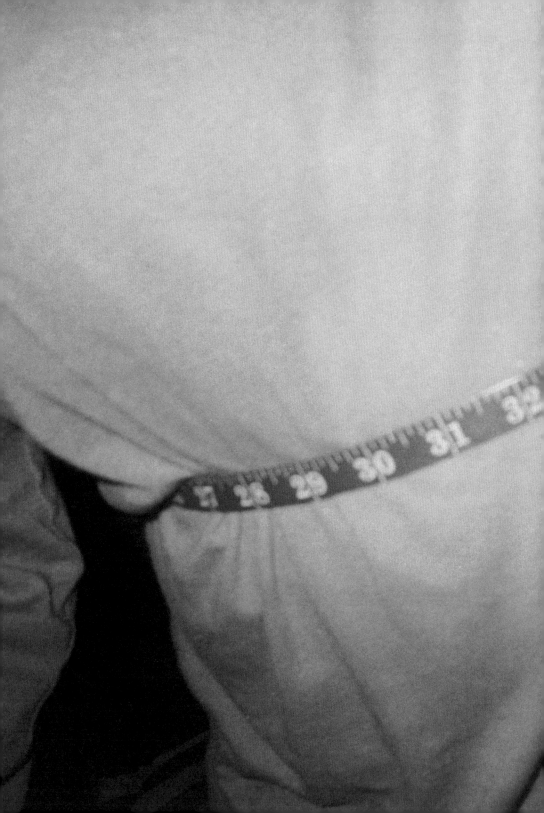

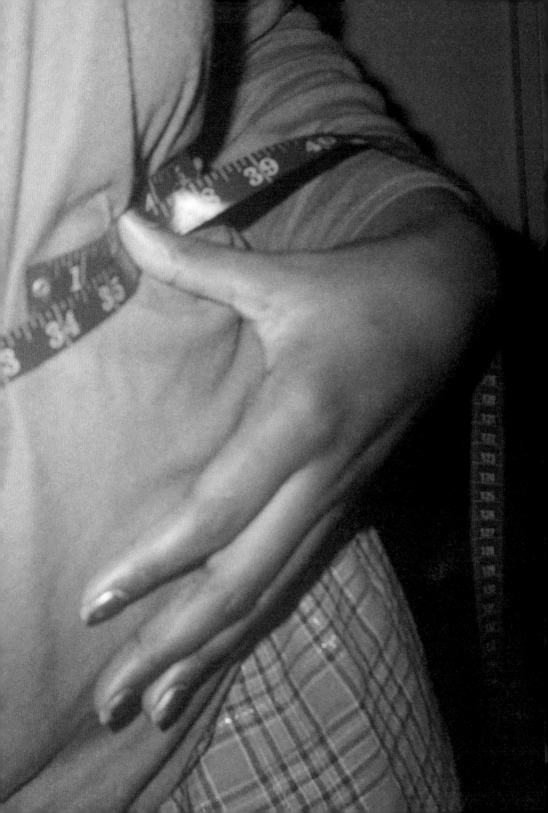

Girls aren't given the orders they observe. They are powerful, influential and can do anything they set their mind too; they are strong in our society.

What are your favorite qualities in a person?

Anyone with a Kind Soul also someone who truely loves what they are doing in life.

Honesty, humor, being Serious who need be, encouraging, fun, don't try to change you

Honesty, Humility,

Personality; basically being able to see how unusual someone is, is Something that I find fun.

Humor, honesty, happiness ... Anything happy ♡ looks dont matter to me.

- sense of humor, how they treat others and me, the way they dress

SENSE of humor, adventurous, spontaneous

Being completely aware of the world around you and being okay with it.

I love people who can make me laugh. I really love people who have that "I dont care about anything" attitude.?

funny, Unpredictable, cool

Sincerety, loyalty, kind

Humor, understanding, accepting, being able to make me feel warm

their humor, loyalty, honesty, awesome personality, intelligence (I love having intellectual conversations)

caring, funny, passionate, responsible.

Responsibility and a sense of humor.

Humor, compassion, enthusiasm, genuinity (urban dictionary)

I love people that can make me laugh and love great
music. I love people that get excited and freakish, weird
like me with me that

THE ABILITY TO HOLD A CONVERSATION
AND INTEREST IN LEARNING. (OUT OF SCHOOL)

someone who does not worry what others think
& they don't obsess over it.

open mind, kind, caring, funny,

Kindness and understanding. I love people who are genuine and understand
that sometimes life can be tough.

sense of humor,

Sense of humor, open-mindedness, creativity, kindness.

individuality, humor, goals

Being able to have a serious conversation,
trustworthyness, caring, fun.

The ability to see good in anyone, being able to admit their mistakes
creative, originality, a fax, math, nshate for everything yet sees
beauty, innocence

Honesty, a good smile, a gregarious nature, thoughtfulness, humor,
decency, quirks.

understanding, forgiving

A good sense of humor.

funny, adventurous, and kindness

Talkative, Happy, Smart, interested in learning, enjoys tea

The ability to say sorry, The ability to laugh, and passion ... for ... something.

SENSE OF HUMOR, ADVENTUROUS, SPONTANEOUS

Trust, adventerous, Funloving, dreamer, stylish.

Generosity & humor & kindness

Kindness, funniness, charismatic, Intresting

they have to be intelligant and witty with a generous heart
and a mind for satire

Honesty, patience, kind, excited, fun, caring, outgoing, loud
caring.

Honesty, if your honest that's amazing. Just putting
your self out there like that is rare & beautiful.

166

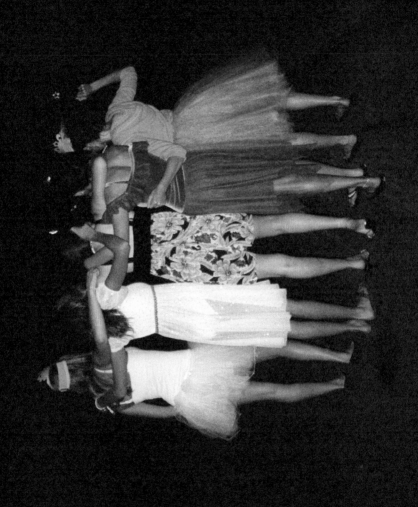

Answering the following questions is not required to participate in The Girl Project, though I would really appreciate your comments. Be as specific as you like. Send in with your camera and release form. Your name is not on this piece of paper and will not be used in conjunction with your identity.

1.) What adjectives best describe you?
confused, loving, teasing, loud, shy, self-councious

2.) What is the hardest part about being a teenager?
-thinking abaut te what I want to do in life, -fitting in but and the fear that I wont accomplish my goals, also standing out at the same time

3.) What is the best part about being a teenager?
- being old enough to roam alone, but too ~~many~~ young to be self-sufficient

4.) What are your favorite qualities in a person?
- sense of humor, how they treat others and me, the way they dress

5.) What is your idea of happiness?
- having money and being surrounded by people who care abaut you / love you

6.) What is your ideal profession?
photographer, photo journalist, lawyer - I am ashamed of being conservative

7.) Tell me one thing about you that nobody else seems to get?
- I am not rich and I can't afford 85% of the things I want so shut up.
- I actually AM overweight and people need to stop telling me otherwise. - I love attention but try to hide it so that I dont look self-centered

8.) What is your favorite color?
PURPLE

9.) If you could live anywhere in the world, where would you live?
London (if I had money), New York city (if I had money), Seattle

10.) What do you think about the way(s) that teenage girls are portrayed in our culture? - we're all portrayed as being obsessed with boys ~~+ boaro~~ not being aware of ov the consequences of our actions

11.) What are you afraid of?
- not living the life I've always wanted - people doing me favors
- not succeeding - being rejected + thinking I'm needy
- losing my grandparents before I can tell them

12.) What are you most proud of?
- getting to States in the NHD competition - getting into a magnet everything middle school
- the photograph I took of my grandma that my family loves

14.) In as many or few words necessary, tell me about being you.
- I regret not ~~the~~ getting into a magnet high school; I feel like I'm slowly becoming dumber as my high school career progresses
- I love my grandparents and I'm scared that any day now, they will pass away without giving me something to pass onto future generations →

- I wish I was more outgoing when I first meet people so that I was more popular & accepted

- I obsess over my skin way too much and I tweeze my eyebrows too much

- I'm hairy

- I desperately want to be rich & powerful/influential

- I would LOVE to go to art school, but I know my parents would never approve/pay for it.

- I want to prove to my parents that my interest in photography is not a waste.

- I'm scared that I'm not doing enough in high school to get into my dream schools ★: georgetown or NYU

- I idolize Edie Sedgwick and want to live a fabulous life like her (but without the overdose-on-drugs part)

- I'm always friends with girls who are hotter versions of me so I can never get guys

- I've never been kissed & I feel prude & ashamed

- I don't drink & do drugs, but I do really want to try both at

- I wish I was considered "hot" and "sexy"

- I wish I was skinny & pretty, so that I could be effortless in the way I look

- There's probably a thousand more facts/confessions about me but I can't think of them.

- Sorry this didn't come in by April 15th. One week is too little time.

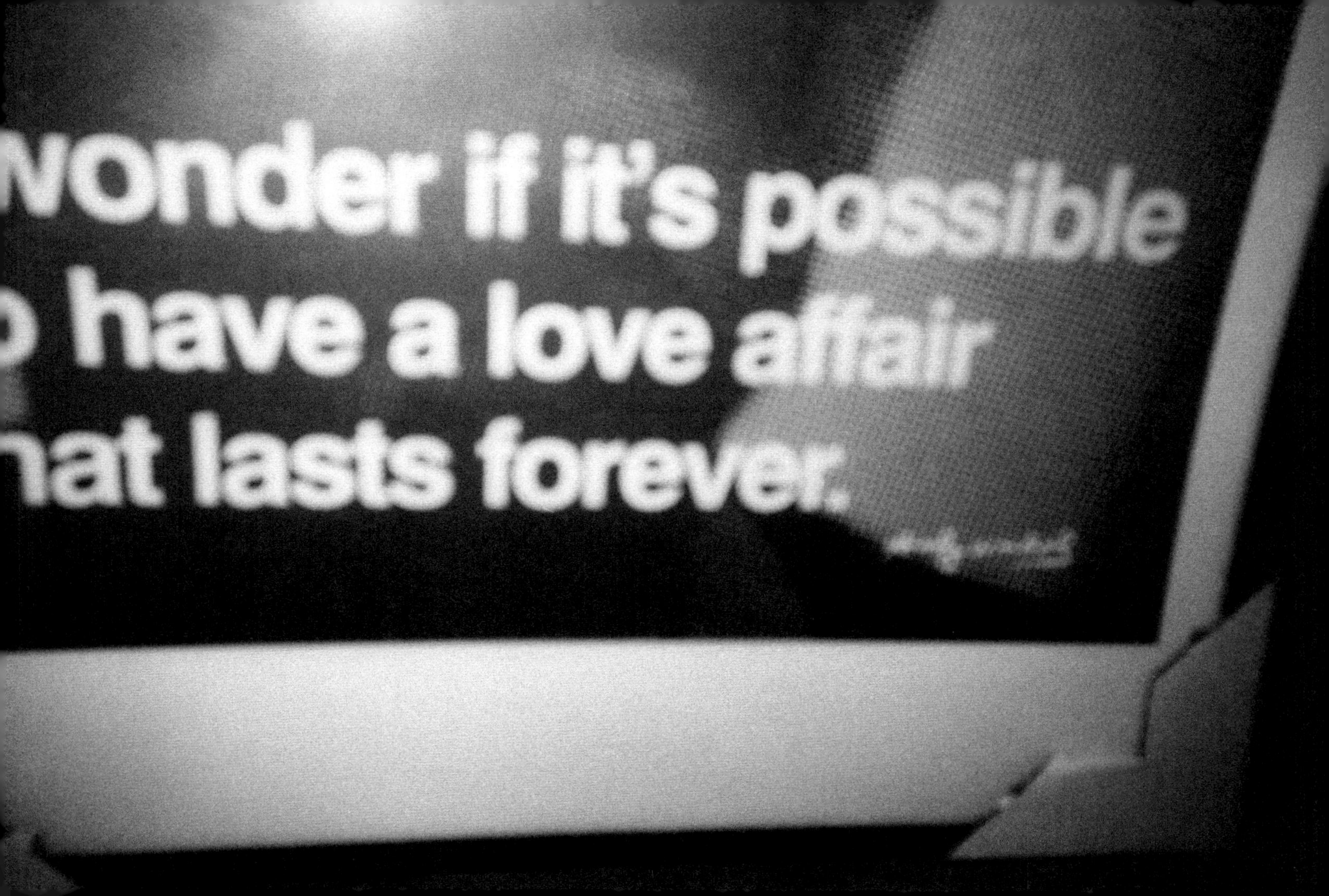

wonder if it's possible

have a love affair

that lasts forever.

every time I make a wish, on an eyelash or a shooting star, or a birthday candle, I always wish for romance and love.

...see it, and I almost hope you don't. But... Sweetie, today marks the One year anniversary of me realizing that I'm in love with you. And I don't think I can ever tell you myself. I am a bisexual 15 year old girl, I've fallen for my best friend, Kate... I LOVE YOU.

Answering the following questions is not required to participate in The Girl Project, though I would really appreciate your comments. Be as specific as you like. Send in with your camera and release form. Your name is not on this piece of paper and will not be used in conjunction with your identity.

1.) What adjectives best describe you?

tenacious

2.) What is the hardest part about being a teenager?

Dealing with yourself: What you think of yourself, what you think boys are doing to you, what you think others think of you, and getting over all of it

3.) What is the best part about being a teenager?

having free time to hang out with friends, drive alone, and be happy!

4.) What are your favorite qualities in a person?

The way they care about other people's happiness and concerns — their empathy, and their humor.

5.) What is your idea of happiness?

Knowing what life is all about, and being able to accept anything that comes to you because then you will know no fear and be happy

6.) What is your ideal profession?

Traveling to third-world countries and being a doctor there.
I also like photography!

7.) Tell me one thing about you that nobody else seems to get?

My problems with myself — I always tell people how I
think I am such a selfish person and I don't do harm good. But
"No one cares if you're miserable, so you might as well be happy!" — that was
a quote from
Somebody I don't
remember

8.) What is your favorite color? Blue

9.) If you could live anywhere in the world, where would you live?

Tata New Zealand or positively Singapore

our culture? I think that there's a lot of advertising towards teenagers to look, dress, and act a certain way, and I simply have to say, Do whatever you think is cool, and don't be afraid to be different! Uniqueness is something we seem to be losing in this world, and we can change that by going our own way.

11.) What are you afraid of?
I am afraid of not knowing. Some people say "Ignorance is bliss," and in some cases it is. But not knowing what is going on in the world, like poverty and war, or not knowing if someone really needs help, now that is what scares me.

12.) What are you most proud of?
What I have learned, and how I have taken that wonderful knowledge to change my life.

13.) In as many or few words necessary, tell me about being you.
If I have difficulties and challenges, as all people do. But I take those and change them from a brickwall barrier to a hill that I can overcome. I have very sweaty hands, and it causes a lot of personal humiliation. But as soon as I stop thinking about myself and what others think of me, I can forget about my hands and move on to more important things.

Snakes/alligators Plastic or cosmetic surgery Being alone.

being alone   failing   Being alone   a void of my knowledge.

being a failure at life.   Loneliness   losing people I love

I'm afraid of screwing up - BIG TIME! rejection

being unsuccessful)   rejection, not being accepted.

Being alone   Failing myself

marrying someone who is like my dad

Death. Loss.   FAILURE!   People I love dying or me dying.
              Cancer genders   Screwing up

the dark   hospitals.   Lately, failure.

                        Not having children

going blind   Death.   being alone for a while

                                                    and the
being alone   Being stuck in our place forever   dark :)

Balloons. And having nowhere to sit at lunch.

death and losing loved ones.   needles

bad authors and musicians.   the dark   spiders

Growing up.   bugs   leaving the people I knew behind

Not being happy   the future

losing my family

Disappointment.
                    Friends Turning On Me

living in world of complete silence   the dark

                    being hurt again. by a boy.

Not having a strong relationship.   Small spaces   violence   Bugs

being kidnapped & tortured

Death.   I'm most afraid of myself being too fearless and
                    impulsive.

being loved ones

188

Spiders

dying, not married / without having a family

Not getting into college

Losing people.

Being alone while surrounded by people.

Being stranded on an iceberg in the middle of the ocean

spiders.

getting cancer

People thinking I'm a freak

loosing anyone I love

being alone

Not having a good GPA

death

being alone,   not being able to follow my dreams   The dark, death,

elevators

Becoming one of them".

never finding my true love

Failed future.

loosing the ones I love

growing old alone (and the dark)

small dark corners,

my loved ones dying

Not getting into college,

Death,

living in this small town forever

not leaving FL. Dead things.

Not accomplishing my dreams.

rejection   the Post Office.   forgetting

Perpetual unhappiness   stink bugs

    making the wrong long-term decisions

        Spiders   becoming blind

Being forgotten.   loosing my Best friends.

                  Disappointing others.

becoming my mother   gaining weight over the winter.

falling in love again.

my parents finding all of the time.   the World fighting all of the time

clowns

Can I tell you a secret? I'm afraid to fall in love.
To tell someone I love them, it's difficult for me.
I've been w/ my boyfriend for 4 months & still haven't said "I love you."

falling in to The World

Talking on the phone.

Spiders

horses

the unknown.

marriage

spiders

Heights, the dark

being alone   the dark   water.

I am afraid of losing my boyfriend.

I am no longer afraid   the govt   Gaining more Weight

I'm afraid of pretty much everything,
but mostly the future.

SNAKES

darkness Needles,

Homeless People

Judgement

the dark.   Heights   Snakes

The Dark

getting fat

scary horror movies

people The Dark :)

Crowds, Being like my father. Never getting married

Fear itself. My worst fear is being unloved and alone.

Answering the following questions is not required to participate in The Girl
Project, though I would really appreciate your comments. Be as specific as
you like. Write on the back or attach another piece of paper if necessary.
Send in with your camera and release form.
Your name is not on this piece of paper and will not be used in conjunction with your identity.

1.) What adjectives best describe you?
honest, punctual, open-minded, thoughtful, considerate, observant

2.) What is the hardest part about being a teenager?
dealing w/ the current while being expected to plan your entire future

3.) What is the best part about being a teenager?
the sometimes enjoyed freedom of a time before "real" life as they call it begins

4.) What are your favorite qualities in a person?
being genuine, self-assured, and open-minded but w/ an opinion

5.) What is your idea of happiness?
total comfort and understanding — like unspoken moments of love

6.) What is your ideal profession?
A National Geographic photojournalist w/ a Psychology education under my belt

7.) Tell me one thing about you that nobody else seems to get?
I truly LOVE my boyfriend (of 2 years) & he loves me — and that's
Our only basic necessity

8.) What is your favorite color? turquoise

9.) If you could live anywhere in the world, where would you live?
In a village on the Mediterranean coast where you need a donkey & everything
is white

10.) What do you think about the ways/that teenage girls are portrayed in our culture? It is horrible and embarrassing and demeaning—I AM NOT own materialistic dumbo that can only think as far as my dyed hair reaches. I am not confined to a plastered face and product covered skin.

11.) What are you afraid of?

Death. Failed future. Disappointment. But ~~too~~ sometimes I meet people that fit this and I lose Hope.

12.) What are you most proud of?

My self-assurance.

13.) Why did you want to participate in The Girl Project?

I thought it was a great concept—I wanted to have some part. It was much harder than expected to put my life into single frame photos — I feel like I failed my own expectations. ~~asea~~ But I guess that's the beauty of the project— it's real & simple... but...complex...

14.) In as many or few words necessary, tell me about being you.

I spend alot of my time satisfying myself and others with high grades and a certain level of achievement, but I don't center my life around school. My small group of friends consists of a variety of strong personalities who all come together with a similar understanding of sarcasm and humor and escape the—we'll take the liberty to say—stereotypes defined by our classmates. I am completely in love with a boy who recently moved to Dallas for his 1st year in college. We depend on each other (not in a bad way) and ~~we~~ we basically serve ⟳

What is your idea of happiness?

Falling asleep next to your best friend, comfortable jeans, a good book... coffee

Happiness is knowing no matter where you are, how you feel, how you look, etc. that someone out there cares about you.

Play tennis, telling jokes   Being with my friends + family!   What you make it. You make yourself happy.

being with my best & true close people in the world...   content with your surroundings (friends, family, environment, etc.)

Doing what you want to do, with the people you want to do it with; living life to the fullest.

Sunlight and a best friend

total comfort and understanding - like unspoken moments of love

Being with the people you love

Being Able To Do What You Enjoy

No hatred even playful hatred, no negative thoughts and it's always countered with a positive one, and to be free from planning the future and live in the moment.

Being With People You Love

- having money and being surrounded by people who care about you / love you

that feeling when the vibe is nice and the weather is hot and the music sounds good and knowing that theres no place in the world I would rather be than right where I am at that second shining around with my friends

Being completely aware of the world around you and being okay with it.

Right now it's reading my Bible, everytime I go back I find something new and it's peaceful. so I don't have insomnia anymore.

Not caring what others think and being true to YOURSELF. Also, skittles; they're pretty awesome too LOL

Love.

Being somewhere warm and sunny, the ocean just a few feet from my dream house. Just existing there would be true happiness

Being with people who care about me and having my camera in my hands to capture every memory

My idea of happiness is to be able to look in the mirror and be completely satisfied, physically and mentally.

Loving who I am and where I am. No regrets.

self acceptance and seeing the world through a poet's eyes

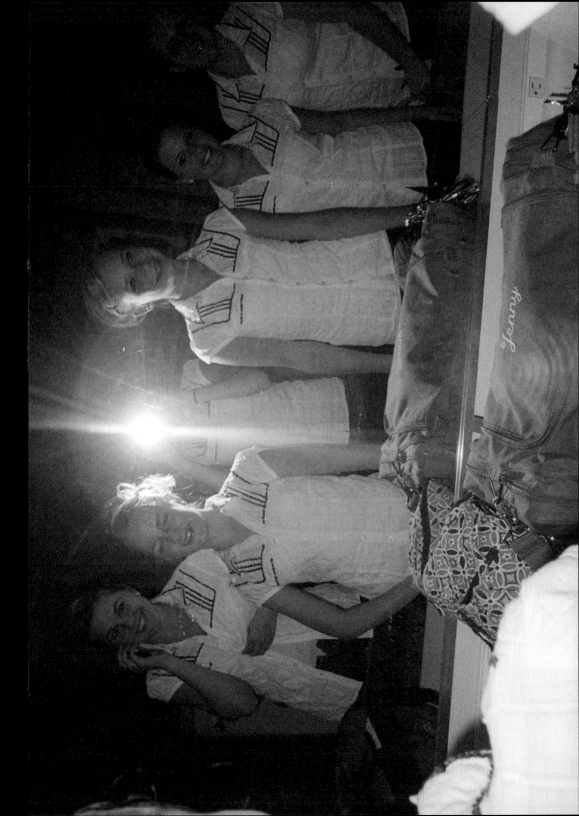

My idea of happiness is to have fun, live in the moment, and make mistakes. Make good mistakes that you'll laugh at and learn from, not mistakes that are illegal or that you'll regret later.

Happiness is being around people you love

being content with where your life is, enjoying the people who surround you, and all around loving that you get to live everyday

Having people or things in your life that can make you smile. Or, overall, being content with yourself.

a sense of calm brought by connecting to others, learning about Disney's Neverland yourself, * doing the activities that _really matter_

Happiness equals the freedom to be who you are without the fear of judgement from others.

Happiness is what makes you truly smile, for me it's being with others who can make me laugh.

true happiness is when you're with people you love and you can't think of anything to worry about because nothing else matters.

My idea of happiness is making others happy. Enjoying beautiful weather while making memories with friends.

New experiences and adventures to keep things exciting. Feeling like I belong.

an endless supply of compact disks, records and itunes - anything with music is happiness

202

Finds you over the period of your life? I think happiness can't look for it, it will just come.

I'm not quite sure.

A life full of friends, family, memories

I think it's everywhere, people just have to try a little harder to see it

Being in a place - physical or mental - where you are completely, utterly content & joyful.

That is a really hard question but I'll try to answer sincerely. I guess it's caring about the ones you love...

Being contented, knowing that you are loved, and seeing sunshine (figurative and literal things apply)

No worries or stress; having the perfect body and being beautiful; marrying an amazing guy who loves me for who I am

Being in love with someone who loves me for me and being surrounded by friends and family.

being with people who love me for me and having my music.

Happiness is being content with who you are and what you have.

freedom. ability to hope for the future.

Achieving contentment with your present situation but not to the point that you don't recognize how you can always better yourself

My idea of happiness is loving myself. Being content with who I am, and my surrounding's Being Care-Free.

falling in love

being with my + best friends lying on the beach playing settlers of catan and yelling at each other till the whole time someone gets so pissed thy thrown me in the ocean + we bodysurf

living you life, being your heart's desire

Being loved

TRAVELING THE WORLD WITH those I love

Having not to worry, being secure about ~~the~~ me ~~ugh~~ ~~+~~ outcome.

Achieving your own success.

Being surrounded by the ones I love ~~could~~ in an enviroment where i can express my true self w/o being judged.

Currently it is Being able to make it through the Day without worring or stressing or getting upset and Being able to Be carefree and enjoy the Day as it is.

Living life happily with the ones you love.

My idea of happiness is being loved by someone, getting an A on an Algebra test, waking up on a cool Saturday morning, and having my favorite pair of jeans washed on dried night.

Answering the following questions is not required to participate in The Girl Project, though I would really appreciate your comments. Be as specific as you like. Send in with your camera and release form. Your name is not on this piece of paper and will not be used in conjunction with your identity.

1.) What adjectives best describe you?

My boyfriend said "Radical, awesome, and beautiful."
I say: Calm, reliable, hardworking, quirky, Kind, quick.

2.) What is the hardest part about being a teenager?

Learning how to handle things like an adult but trying to maintain a fine balance of still being Young and fun.

3.) What is the best part about being a teenager?

★★ Being able to learn all sorts of new things with new experiences ahead of you and opened up for you. Figuring out life with a Yung, strong body all the while making great memories w/ friends and family. ★★

4.) What are your favorite qualities in a person?

★★ *Kindness* Humility. LOVE + HUMOR 3 FUN ☺
UNDERSTANDING!

5.) What is your idea of happiness?

#1) Making God happy. Living a simple but appreciative life and getting married so that I will always have my best friend by my side. ☺ Yeah, thats it. ☺

6.) What is your ideal profession?

Funny you should ask, because photography is and has been my greatest passion for a while now. Something you love is more important than money.

7.) Tell me one thing about you that nobody else seems to get?

OK, well I know that I'm only 17 years old, but I am engaged. Yeah.
Nobody seems to get why I would want to be. Oh well. ☺

☆↝BLACK, YELLOW, GRAY↜☆

9.) If you could live anywhere in the world, where would you live?
🌺 Hawaii OR Tahiti: b/c I want simpler life and have more time for the small things. And I love the whole hiking/outdoors scene !! 💧

10.) What do you think about the way(s) that teenage girls are portrayed in our culture? ★ Sadly we are portrayed a lot of the time as dumb, snooty, ★ careless, slutty, etc... and sadly a lot of the time it could be true. However it makes me happy when we are portrayed as able, creative, level-headed, sweet, smart and accomplished young people. ★★

11.) What are you afraid of?

FAILURE, of course. The FUTURE, at times... Not having love in my life. ◦◦◦◦ †

12.) What are you most proud of?

OVERCOMING some pretty impossible things ANOREXIA, DISSAPPINTING PROVING that I'm a GOOD PERSON to people who once HATED me GOD! and finally being

13.) In as many or few words necessary, tell me about being you.

✸ Broad question, but here we go.... Being me is filled with happy with who I am ♥ so many emotions that are overwhelming. Extreme joy, shock, fury, passion, heartbreak – but the one I focus on above all is Love. I think I have more than many people do, and I'm blessed for that. Being me is enjoyable, exhausting, and interesting. At the same time though, being me is very demanding at yes. Family, friends, and teachers all expect a great deal from me because they now I can handle it. That doesn't always make it any easier, though. ⟶

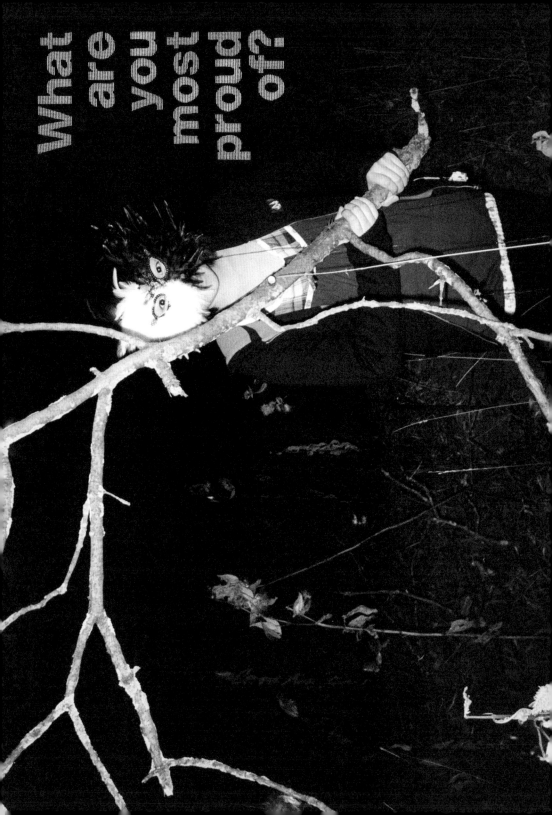

What are you most proud of?

People trust me. My self-assurance. My photogaphy that I take with
my EasyShare 2915 Kodak camera. How I've changed, & how
I'll keep changing.

My self - esteem and baby brother/godson.

My wonderful boyfriend.

My ability to surprise myself w/ doing well, learning, Activism and all
the people who devote their lives to if, Driving

Quite

MAKING MYSELF PLEASE MY PASSION FOR PHOTOGRAPHY
By DEFYING MY PARENTS AND ARRYING TO INTERCEDEN AND NYU.

My mother. My accomplishments.

That I dress the way I want to, not the way others want
me to. That I feel comfortable with myself, no matter if I'm wearing
a dress and combat boots or sweat pants

speak my ability to
speak my mind.

That I know I'm smart even if I say I don't

My patience

My interests and opinions. I want to show people + the world
through my eyes.

I'm proud of being the first in my family to
go to a four year university. I worked hard to My compashion for others
get the money to go. College was my dream.
graduating high school

going to a great Art school & getting A lot of
scholarships to be able to go there

The fact that I've survived this far. Yes, I have attempted suicide twice been to rehab, but I have risen above and I'm pretty proud of that.

I don't think I am proud of anything. I guess I am proud of where my family has come, and about having a beautiful glorious for Ashley, but, I have still yet to find what makes me proud.

My artistic talents

being able to pay for my own gas, movies, food & clothes with out asking my rents for money. I like being independent. I'm also proud of being a vegetarian

My accomplishments in dance, I'm a pre-proffession.

The life that God has brought into my hands.

the fact that I am myself

I'm most proud of myself for having the time of my life at this age, I really do love my life.

my attention to detail.

My accomplishments so far

The things I have accomplished
And surviving being a teenage girl so far.

212

staying true to myself after moving from another country

Staying on top with my studies / staying above the influence

My ability to be "stay "good". Being a generaly good person

myself. I think I'm beautiful and I can do anything.

I'm proud that I've grown to be an independent young woman who is self sufficient and knows her worth as the best there my ability to be lovable is when I dedicate myself to something. ♡

my grades....

My good grades. My family.

oh and my chest.

My art and my singing.
Also how my advice seems to ACTUALLY help people.

I'm proud of being intelligent. I'm proud of who I have become and who I am becoming.

Managing to be myself, even though I was different from the other girls at my high school

My compassion - I love how invested I get in things

The fact that I overcame my father abandoning my family.
That I am a strong person, with an even stronger will to live.

Who Iam. Iam most proud of my heritage; Native American, my group of friends
African American, Caucasian, and everything imaginable. Its just who I am.

Being aware. Knowing about how the world works outside my mind and
knowing I can help change it if I try.

My involvement with charity. As cheesy as
it sounds, it really makes me so grateful and appreciative

Being a MUSLIM teenage girl in America

my morals and the extent to which I live by them

My Photography. To look at a picture I took and say "that's MINE"
"I made it. And it's beautiful."

my resistance to peer pressure   that I am alcohol free and Drug free. I Do good in school.
I've stuck to my morals and values, even with
all the peer pressure.

I am most proud of my musical talents. I can play piano,
bass guitar, some percussion instruments, and I can sing.
without my musical abilities, I wouldn't be me or have
anything to live for

my progress in photography. music, english and   That I've finally found who I am, and I love myself.
theatre. Being a generally genuinely moral person.

The person that I am today. I may not be perfect, but I live my
life in a positive way. I love my friends and family, I'm dedicated to   being myself.
the hobbies I enjoy (like music), and all around, a nice person.

Not being closed minded in a judgmental community

My inwards is complex, my outwards is very simple.
I don't like being alone with my own mind, I love being
surrounded by a friend's laughter. I try to drown myself
and others in positivity, because that is the best way
to be.

Chloe Conn
Mia Bomar
Regine Vencer
Kaitlin Wachsberger
Ariel Caldwell
Kate Schneider
Aidaly Sanchez
Amanda Latta
Jude Garcia
Jasmine Lowe
Annie Fichtner
Brooke Fortune
Chelsea Hollenbeck
Justina Wong
Alisa Greene
Erin Sornsin
Taylor Gonzalez
Ebony Enabulele

Maryam Abdul-Kareem
Beatrice Schachenmayr
Ana Opishinski
Suzanne Maroney
Rachel Fitzgerald
Revelle Gerson
Bailey Mulholland
Aysha Banos
Tyler Ann Numley
Marissa Meltzer
Jude Garcia
Jenny Fox
Gillian Baker
Katie Roetker
Ximena Izquierdo
Emily Gramajo
Michelle Segroves
Shell Feda

Yasmina Marth
Amber Anderson
Hannah Stephanie Lem-
kowitz
Mary Resler
Maria S. Iqbal
Katie Thompson
Miranda Mortensen
Carly Starnes
Maddie Hagan
Tatianna Flores
Ashley Faulkner
Catherine Aviles
Yaritsa Carrasco
Surya Ry
Courtney Craig
Kayla Delacerda
Alelie Adriano

Olivia Locher
Cristin Franks
Yanni Garcia
Olivia Locher
Lauren Utech
Vera Casagrande
Marissa List
Tarah Dawdy
Christina Wolf
Heather Evans
Theresa L. Miller
Alex Linares
Ashley Arias
Keana Flanders
Nora May
Jordan Blakeley
Christine Waters
Jenna Cheung

Evelyn Padilla
Melissa Wood
Samantha Haynes
Amy Packett
Ally Mac
Lauren Held
Sammy Brodsky
Ashley Van Speybroeck
Danielle Chudolij
Liz Lorenz
Mary Resler
Jordana Approvato
Destiny Rosales
Valerie White
Stephanie "Effie" Hobbins
Stephanie Perry
Lexi Patton
Marcy Hernandez
Ishobel Pomrening
Kristen Clinton
Anna Marten
Sammy Brodsky
Jenny Fox

Elizabeth Doyle
Alexandra Linn
Brenna Levitin
Gabriella Alziari
Ana Maria Velasquez
Sarah Ching
Katie Hanright
Lindsay McCoy
Gloria Oduyoye
Emma Carlson
Shell Feda
Lily Greene
Ashley Carroll
Marie Taylor
Amy Packett
Alli DeFeo
Jordan Blakeley
Ana Maria Velasquez
Bobbie-Jean Fisher
Boys and Girls Club of
Venice
Jori Remus
Jessica Farrah

Barbara Cawley
Ashley Plocha
Emma Van Akkeren
Katie Ohman
Gloria Oduyoye
Rachel Kazaryan
Carmesi Sanchez
Courtney Craig
Kate Schneider
Carly Starnes
Jessica Cain
Sloane Wolter
Haley Reese-Gawthhorne
Savannah Dean
Anderson Toups
Anonymous
Monica Quiroz
Hannah Walsh
Olivia Locher
Eva Preciado
Paige Meisenheimer
Abby Ruffer
Shelley Rodriguez

Christine Waters
Stacey Bear
Monica Salazar
Melissa Valencia
Liz Lorenz
Morgan Cole
Revelle Gerson
Olivia Locher
Taylor Gonzalez
Mercedes Bleth
Jessica Farrah
Catherine Aviles
Rachel Lezthe
Mckenzie Barnum
Ashley Plocha
Beatriz Camino
Annie Fichtner
Lisa Zhou
Anderson Toups
Olivia Curry
Karlie Valer
Lindsay McCoy
Linh Huynh

P.S. I hope you enjoy my photos of me, my friends, and the beautiful world I am so lucky to be living in.

thank you

to all participants of The Girl Project.
I am grateful for your insights and creativity.

Thank you to all friends of The Girl Project. Your support has been an inspiration. Special thanks to the young women of the Lower East Side Girls Club, Girls Inc., and Boys and Girls Clubs of America. Thank you to the SCOPE Foundation and Kodak for your support of the project. Thank you to CRC/Vista Imaging Group and Proof Digital for your photo services. Thank you to Daniel Power, Cecilia Dean, and Anne Pasternak for your advice and willingness to share your contacts. Thank you to everyone at Rizzoli, especially Martynka Wawrzyniak, Charles Miers, and Juliette Cezzar. THANK YOU TGP INTERNS: Elyssa Marcus, Chassey Reyes, Kim Clancy, and Madeline Porsella — you ladies are the best. Extra-special thanks to my parents, Jerry and Verla Engelbrecht, and my brother, Judd Engelbrecht. Also to Kristin (Liebel) Poteet for so many wonderful girlhood memories and years of friendship. Most importantly, thank you to Jed Walentas, my supportive, patient, and generous husband. Without you, The Girl Project would not have been possible.

First published in the United States of America in 2011
by Rizzoli International Publications, Inc.
300 Park Avenue South
New York, NY 10010
www.rizzoliusa.com

Edited by Martynka Wawrzyniak
Designed by Juliette Cezzar / e.a.d.

© 2011 Kate Engelbrecht & The Girl Project
Text © 2011 Kate Engelbrecht & The Girl Project

2011 2012 2013 2014 / 10 9 8 7 6 5 4 3 2 1

Distributed in the U.S. trade by Random House, New York

Printed in China
ISBN: 978-0-7893-2260-9

Library of Congress Control Number: 2011922166

The images and texts in this book have been randomly placed by the author. The reader should not assume that the paired writings and photographs are by the same girls or intended to suggest this.